An Introduction to
Islamic Arms

COVER ILLUSTRATION
a Miquelet gun, Turkish 18th century
b Miquelet pistol, Caucasian 19th century
c Saddle-axe Indo-Persian 18/19th century
d Gun barrel, Persian dated 1810
e Dagger, Turkish late 17th century
f Sword, Saudi-Arabian 19/20th century

Frontispiece
Akbar at the battle of Sanai,
1572
Illustration from the
Akbarnama
Indian (Mughal) about 1590
20.1 × 32 cm IS 2-1896 106/117

An Introduction to

Islamic Arms

Anthony North
Research Assistant, Department of Metalwork
Victoria & Albert Museum

LONDON: HER MAJESTY'S STATIONERY OFFICE

Series editor Julian Berry
Designed by HMSO Graphic Design
Printed in England for Her Majesty's Stationery Office

ISBN 0 11 290384 3
Dd 718121 C65

Acknowledgements
I should like to express my thanks to my colleagues Mrs Shirley Bury, for
her helpful comments on the text, and Dr Oliver Watson for his help with
translation.
I owe a considerable debt to Mr K. Jackson for his excellent photography.

A.R.E. North
April 1984

HER MAJESTY'S STATIONERY OFFICE

Government Bookshops

49 High Holborn, London WC1V 6HB
13a Castle Street, Edinburgh EH2 3AR
9-21 Princess Street, Manchester M60 8AS
Southey House, Wine Street, Bristol BS1 2BQ
258 Broad Street, Birmingham B1 2HE
80 Chichester Street, Belfast BT1 4JY

Government publications are also available
through booksellers

The full range of Museum publications is displayed and sold at
The Victoria and Albert Museum, South Kensington, London SW7 2RL.

Introduction

Unlike Western arms the styles and shapes of Islamic arms did not continually change. Once an Islamic armourer had found a satisfactory design, it was often retained for many centuries. The swords and daggers now worn as part of traditional Arab dress differ only slightly from those carried in the 15th century. The attraction of Islamic arms for the collector and scholar is to be found not only in their elaborate decoration but also in the problems they pose. Many bear inscriptions which have to be deciphered and the arms themselves may be of unusual design or made from unfamiliar materials.

In the field of firearms the Arabs made a significant contribution at an early stage. It was principally due to the work of Arab chemists that the knowledge of gunpowder as a propellant was transmitted from China to the West in the 13th century. Curiously Islamic gunsmiths were content to manufacture firearms of comparatively simple mechanism and design until recent times.

The use of watered steel in the manufacture of Islamic arms and armour produces the beautiful surface texture so much admired by collectors. Islamic craftsmen were by no means restricted by the intractable material in which they worked. Gun barrels were chiselled in the form of monsters, sword-hilts were forged in complicated shapes and dagger hilts were made from carved hardstones. It is the variety of design and decoration coupled with their practicality that makes a study of the work of Islamic armourers so rewarding.

Many of the large collections of Islamic arms to be found in European museums were formed in the 19th century by enthusiasts for Eastern art like Henri Moser-Charlottenfels, whose collection is now in the Berne Historical Museum, or Lord Hertford, whose collection is now in Hertford House, London. These wealthy collectors acquired Eastern arms not on the basis of their historical interest, but for their lavish decoration and unusual form. The arms display every facet of Eastern decoration but most of them date from after the 17th century.

Although there are descriptions in contemporary inventories of arms brought to the West from the Holy Land by Crusaders, hardly any appear to have survived. Contrary to expectation Islamic arms from the period of the Crusades — the 11th and 12th centuries — are represented in collections by only a few miserable fragments. At a later period, in the 16th and 17th centuries, Islamic arms are depicted in Western European paintings, but usually only as exotic furnishings. Wherever the West came into direct military conflict with Islam such as in Eastern Europe, a rich legacy of Islamic arms is to be found. Constant warfare throughout the 15th, 16th and 17th centuries led to a substantial amount of captured stores finding their way into the arsenals of Eastern Europe. The Imperial arms collections in Vienna contain some fine Turkish and Persian arms of the 15th and 16th centuries. In Great Britain the legacy of Empire brought large quantities of arms from Islamic lands to these shores. Most of them are, however, of disappointingly late date. However the East India Company had the pick of several important Indian arsenals from the 18th century such as Tanjore and Lahore. As a result some of the finest and some of the earliest Islamic arms came to this country through the agency of the Company and are now safe in the Victoria and Albert Museum.

Many arms found their way to the West when the old-established princely arsenals were broken up in the 18th and 19th centuries. A substantial number of early pieces from the important arsenal of St. Irene in Istanbul became separated from the main collections or were sold to collectors in the first half of the 19th century. As nearly all the arms from the arsenal were incised with an inventory mark, the original contents can be traced. The Istanbul arsenal contained a large number of Egyptian and Syrian items, formely in Cairo, which were presumably taken as booty at the battle of Chaldiran 1514, or Ridanya 1517, when Selim the Grim (1512-1520) defeated the Mameluks.

A number of 14th-and 15th-century European swords are preserved in the Askeri Museum, Istanbul, that were formerly in the St. Irene arsenal. These are inscribed on the blade with details of their deposition in the arsenal at Alexandria. Originally of Italian manufacture, some of these are known to have been captured by the Mameluks in their attack on Cyprus in 1426, then taken by the Turks from Alexandria to Istanbul.

Islam represents a huge geographical area comprising a multitude of different cultures. Each had its individual national type of weapons. Craftsmen often worked far from the area where they learned their trade, either voluntarily or under duress. It is recorded, for example, that Tamerlane transported armourers and swordsmiths from Damascus to his new capital Samarkand in 1400. Valuable blades and gun-barrels were often re-mounted many times by different craftsmen so any inscription on the blade or barrel may not necessarily relate to the date of the hilt or gun-stock.

As in the West, arms designed as regalia or for parade were often styled after archaic models. Certain types of Persian spear made in the form of tridents are clearly of 19th-century manufacture, yet reflect a medieval shape.

One of the chief sources of delight that the 19th-century collectors found in Islamic arms was their lavish decoration. Nearly every example is richly inlaid with gold or silver. Swords are fitted with gold hilts and silver scabbards; guns are covered with delicate enamelled gold mounts and daggers are fitted with hilts carved of precious stones. Decoration can range from crude, heavy plain gold mounts to finely worked arabesques and flowers. In many cases the utility and function of a particular weapon are subordinated to its decoration. A richly mounted dagger or sword is often fitted with a blade of indifferent quality.

One of the characteristics of Islamic armourer's work is the use of what is known as 'watered' steel. The surface of the steel presents an appearance rather like 'moiré' silk with a pattern of wavy lines meandering over the surface (plate 1). Watered steel was made from ingots of steel containing a very high carbon content. Particles of iron carbide formed the light areas which contrasted with the darker areas of carbon. The structural pattern of the metal was brought out by etching. The ingots came in the form of flat cakes known as 'wootz' and from these the smith forged a blade to the required shape. A skilful smith was able to forge a blade so that the surface pattern followed a particular design. The well-known 'Muhammad's ladder' pattern presents a series of transverse 'rungs' along the entire length of the blade. This was produced by cutting horizontal grooves with a chisel across the blade then forging the blade flat. The Islamic smith could produce a variety of patterns and colours ranging from almost straight 'watering' to small circular 'pools'. Colours range from black to a sulphurous yellow, depending upon what acid was used in the etching process. There are references[1] for the use of watered steel from the 6th century AD. By the 19th century it was used to make a variety of objects ranging from vases to figures of animals.

The museum's collection of Islamic arms was formed mainly in the 19th century. It was assembled to demonstrate decoration rather than typology. Although many of the arms date from the 18th or 19th centuries, the fine condition and high quality of decoration makes the collection one of the most important for any study of the subject.

1
Section of a blade
'Watered' in the pattern known as
Muhammad's ladder
Persian, 17th century

1. Smith C.S., *A History of Metallography*, p. 6, Chicago 1965

Islamic Firearms

Although Arab alchemists knew about gunpowder as a substance through their contacts with China by the first half of the 13th century, firearms were first developed in the West. There are references in an Arab manuscript describing and illustrating primitive handguns. These are called 'midfa' and consisted of a wooden tube mounted on a pole, which was loaded with gunpowder and fired either arrows or bullets. However the manuscript which illustrates this primitive gun, is a late 15th-century copy of a much earlier work and possibly contains added material. It cannot therefore be cited as a primary source[2].

Turkey

Dr Zygulski has pointed out in his important survey of Islamic firearms that the Turks were among the first countries of Islam to fully appreciate the military value of firearms[3]. The effective use of cannon at the siege of Constantinople in 1453 is well known and it seems likely that Turkish troops were equipped with firearms by 1500. Janissaries — the crack troops employed by the Sultans — are depicted in illuminated manuscripts dating from the first half of the 16th century with matchlock muskets of a distinctive shape. A janissary holding a matchlock with a round barrel and square sectioned stock with downward curve is shown in an engraving published in Antwerp in 1576 in the *Navigatione et viaggi nel le Turchia* by Nicolai del Delpinato. Both these constructional characteristics can be seen on surviving Turkish guns. For reasons that remain unclear Eastern gunsmiths virtually ignored the invention of the wheel-lock and remained firmly attached to the matchlock and snap-lock mechanisms, most probably because of their reliability and simplicity.

There are a number of matchlock guns preserved in Eastern European collections which could be dated to the 16th century. However as matchlocks continued to be used until very much later, their early date cannot be confirmed. There are some interesting dated and datable guns preserved in the Dresden Historisches Museum that had been captured from the Turks[4]. One with a combined match and miquelet

2. *Pollards History of Firearms.* Editor C. Blair, p. 25, London 1983
3. Op. cit. p. 425
4. Dresden Historisches Museum Y.311

lock carries an inscription recording its capture from a Turkish janissary in 1683. Others are described in some of the late 17th-century
inventories so their dates are established.

The snap-lock mechanism known as the 'miquelet' was eagerly
adopted by the Turks, sometime in the first half of the 17th century.
The construction of this lock is comparatively simple consisting of an
external mainspring, two screws operating through the lock plate to
allow half-cock and full-cock, and a steel and pan-cover which are
combined. Fashionable in Spain and Italy by the early 17th century,
the miquelet lock was carried to North Africa from Spain. The Turks
presumably obtained their early miquelet locks through Arab traders
and then commenced to make their own versions. The stout construction and lack of complication which permitted repairs to be easily
made no doubt led to the continuing popularity of this form of lock
for nearly two hundred years. Characteristic of Turkish made miquelets are steels with deep vertical grooves and a distinctively shaped
cock.

By 1700 imported locks operating on the flintlock principle tended
to replace the miquelet. The majority of these flintlocks came from
Western Europe but Turkish flintlocks were made locally — these,
like the miquelets, can usually be distinguished by their vertically
grooved steels.

Turkish gun barrels with their characteristic watering were highly
prized even in the West, and are often found mounted by the best
European gunmakers. A fine long Turkish barrel is fitted to one of the
muskets from Louis XIII's 'cabinet d'armes'[5]. Turkish gun barrels
were generally made with very thick walls of round and polygonal
section. The thickness permitted craftsmen to chisel designs deeply
into the surface without in any way affecting the strength of the barrel.
Large areas were sometimes chiselled away leaving interlaced arabesques and palmettes in relief. Certain 17th-century barrels have
wide tulip shaped muzzles. Many Turkish barrels gradually expanded
towards the muzzle, with stepped mouldings near the breech. Both
smooth-bore and rifled barrels are found, the rifling being generally
deep and straight. Another distinctive feature is the prominent back-
sight. In the 17th and early 18th centuries this is in the form of a raised
plate pierced with a series of apertures lining up with a bead sight at the
muzzle.

Very large wall guns were a speciality of Turkish gun-makers and a
fine series is preserved in Topkapi Palace in Istanbul. These have very
thick long barrels, the muzzles sometimes deeply chiselled in the form
of monster's heads or with repeating foliate patterns. Gold inlay was
often used to decorate barrels. The surface was sometimes cut away
and gold set into the barrel or narrow wires of gold and silver were
hammered into the surface.

By the 17th century a characteristic stock shape had been devel-

5. Victoria and Albert Museum No. 12-1949 No. 3 in the French Royal Inventory

2

2
a Miquelet carbine
The stock set with brass mosaics and ivory, the barrel of watered steel
Turkish, 18th century
100 cm   M.389-1924

b Miquelet carbine
The stock set with brass mosaics, the rifled barrel of watered steel, the lock inlaid with engraved brass
Turkish, late 17th century
89.5 cm   971-1884

3
a Miquelet gun
The stock set with ivory inlaid with mosaic, the watered steel barrel overlaid with engraved gold, the lock mounted with coral and overlaid with gold
Turkish, 18th century
119 cm   978-1884

b Miquelet gun
The stock mounted in ivory, set with mosaics, mother o'pearl and imitation stones set in engraved silver; the barrel chiselled and overlaid with gold
Turkish, 18th century
153.5 cm   406-1874

4
a Miquelet gun
The stock inlaid with ivory, mother o'pearl and mosaic, with mounts of engraved silver-gilt; the rifled barrel of watered steel overlaid in gold with verses. The barrel bears the signature of the maker 'Ahmad'
Turkish, 18th century
147 cm   M.49-1946

b Miquelet rifle
The stock overlaid with engraved silver and mounted in ivory, the rifled barrel overlaid in gold
Turkish, about 1800
151 cm   M.48-1946

oped. This was polygonal and straight with a substantial step just behind the breech. The butt was often formed as a separate element from a large block of ivory joined to the main stock by dowels. The surface of the stock was decorated in a variety of ways. Pierced and engraved silver sheet was applied to the surface (not dissimilar to the work found on certain Spanish guns); coral, mother-of-pearl and various metals were inlaid into the stock; velvet was pinned to the surface with decorative studs; some 17th-and early 18th-century Turkish guns were set with a characteristic form of mosaic formed of brass and horn. Inlay was a speciality of Turkish woodworkers and it seems likely that the stocks were sent to specialist craftsmen for decoration.

Initially the barrels were attached to the stocks by pins passing through lugs under the barrel but by the 17th century a different method of attachment had been devised which became almost universally employed by Eastern gunsmiths. Wide bands of metal known as capucines were slipped over the barrel and stock to hold them together. These bands varied in number depending on the length of the barrel, six to eight being the usual number. They were made from embossed silver sheet and were shaped to fit the profile of barrel and stock.

Western gunmaking techniques had a substantial influence on Turkish craftsmen as one would expect. Turkish barrel makers seem to have been specially impressed with the barrels produced by the

3

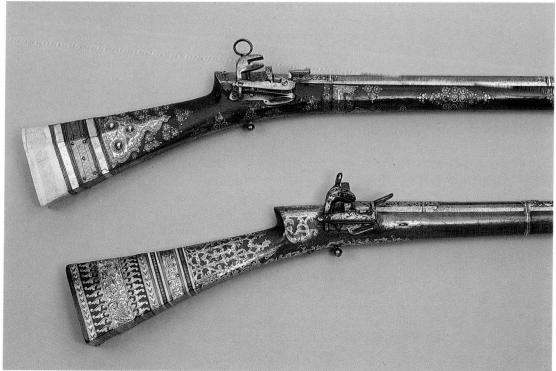

4

Cominazzo family of Northern Italy. Genuine Cominazzo barrels were highly prized in Europe and it is likely that their reputation found its way to Turkey. The Turkish barrel makers took up the name and proceeded to engrave it into their barrels in order to pass their work off as that of the Cominazzo family. Many Turkish guns are inscribed LAZARI COMINAZ or simply bear a cheerful set of squiggles in a gallant attempt at a European name.

Turkish gunmakers signed their guns in a variety of ways. Lock-plates are often stamped with a name, barrels are inlaid with names and dates, and sometimes the name of an owner. The silver mounts are also occasionally stamped with a Tughra, the calligraphic cypher used during the reign of each Sultan. During the 18th century, many Turkish locks were engraved with pseudo-European lettering imitating the signatures found on European flintlocks.

The gun was always the preferred firearm in Turkish lands, although other forms of firearms were used. A number of Turkish blunderbusses are to be found, probably introduced from the Continent at some time in the 18th century. These have the standard bell-shaped muzzle and short stock of European forms. The stocks are inlaid with scrolling wire and resemble the short Spanish blunder-busses of the early 18th century which were almost certainly their ancestors. Although the butts are shaped to fit, their small proportions make them about impossible to shoot from the shoulder, and it has been suggested that they were used from the hip when on horseback[6].

Pistols were apparently used from the 17th century but the majority of surviving examples date from the 18th and 19th centuries. Fitted with either miquelet or flint locks these were made in several forms. They can roughly be divided into those made in an indigenous Turkish style and those under Western influence. Features of the first group include a curious rat-tail stock, the use of embossed silver sheet over the entire surface, and an extended tubular capucine at the muzzle. By far the most common are those made under Western influence. Their shape follows the standard form with down-curving stock and prominent butt. Some late 18th-century types follow German styles with a small curved butt and carved stock. Others have the profile of Spanish and Italian flintlock pistols of the mid 18th century but are covered with intricate floral scroll-work or have stocks formed of silver sheet with cast details.

One very unusual pair of Turkish flintlocks with chiselled steel mounts, seems to be based on Italian late 17th-century prototypes. The lock plate is engraved with pseudo-European lettering and the steel mounts are chiselled with masks and curious skirted figures. The masks closely resemble Brescian chiselled steel work and would be attributed to an Italian hand were it not for the curious engraving. Either the Turkish craftsmen copied an Italian pistol or had access to a Brescian pattern book. The former seems more plausible. In style

6. Blair C., *Pistols of the World,* p. 65, London 1968

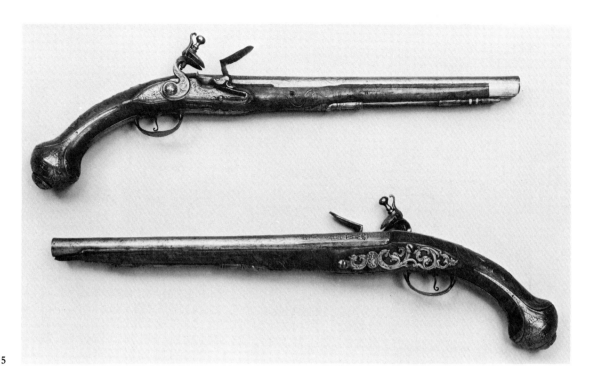

5
Pair of flintlock pistols
The mounts of chiselled steel, the stocks of walnut inlaid with silver wire
These were probably copied from Italian originals
Turkish, about 1690 or later
52.5 cm   Acquired in Cyprus   1568-1888

these date from the late 17th century but they were possibly made much later. They were acquired in Cyprus in the late 19th century.

Filigree work was sometimes employed to decorate pistol stocks. A pair of percussion pistols are illustrated with the entire stocks covered in filigree with cast details imitating precious stones. These seem to date from about 1800, the percussion locks being a replacement of about 1830.

The subject of Turkish pistols cannot be concluded without mentioning those made in Western Europe designed for the Turkish market. Throughout the 18th century there was a considerable demand from Turkey for objects made by European craftsmen in a vivid Oriental manner. Clocks, watches and firearms were especially popular. In the late 18th and early 19th century French gunmakers made a large number of firearms exclusively for the Turkish market. Characteristics include elaborate silver mounts, floral inlay in the stock and embossed trophies. The decorative motifs usually include turbans, crescents and Eastern arms.

The influence of Turkish styles of gunmaking spread far beyond the

6

6
A pair of percussion pistols. The barrels of chiselled watered steel, the locks overlaid with silver, the stocks covered with silver filigree set with coral. Turkish, about 1820.   54.0 cm 1226-1888

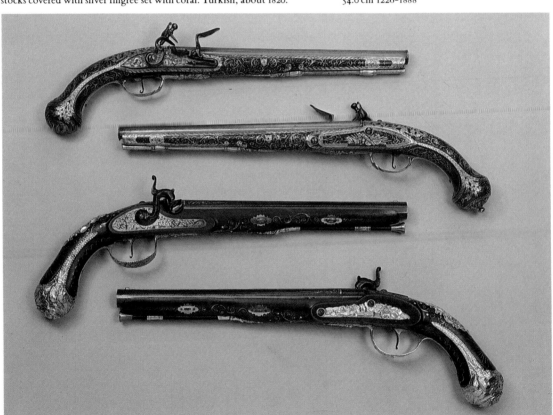

7

7

a Pair of flintlock pistols
The mounts of engraved silver, the
stocks set with silver wire and
engraved panels, the barrels inscribed
'Lazari Cominaz'
Turkish, about 1740
49.5 cm   M.460-1910

b Pair of percussion pistols
The mounts of engraved blued steel
and embossed silver, the stocks set
with silver wire and mother o' pearl,
the barrels inlaid with gold.
The flamboyant silver mounts
embossed with eastern motifs indicate
that these were designed for the
Turkish market
French, about 1840
50.5 cm   Circ. 194-1916

8

a Miquelet pistol
The watered steel barrel engraved and
inlaid with gold, the lock overlaid
with gold, the stock of silver-gilt and
niello
Caucasus (Daghestan) about 1840
41 cm   723-1889

b Miquelet pistol
The watered steel barrel chiselled and
overlaid with gold, the lock overlaid
with gold, the stock of silver-gilt and
niello
Caucasus (Daghestan) about 1840
47 cm   M.630-1911

borders of Turkey. Some of the most interesting firearms from a decorative point of view were produced in those areas such as the Balkans,
which had been under Turkish domination since the 16th century.
Here influences of both East and West were brought to bear on the
craft. Before the 17th century firearms and elements of firearms were
imported but by the middle of the 17th century, various native Balkan
firearms can be recognised. In Bosnia and Serbia a type of gun known
as a 'Sisana' was used. This closely resembled Turkish prototypes and
had a characteristic butt shape. In contrast a very light long gun called
a 'Tancica' was produced in Albania, Montenegro and Yugoslavia
during the 18th century. The butt has a distinctive fish-tail stock of
hardwood mounted in iron. The top of the breech is set with rect-
angular plaques of mother-of-pearl or brass and the underside of the
stock from breech to muzzle is sheathed in iron engraved with sub-
Islamic motifs. The long light barrels were either imported from Italy
or were based on Italian models. The miquelet locks have a characteristic wide top jaw of spatulate form usually decorated with groov-
ing. Another typically Balkan firearm was the 'Rasak', a long gun
with fish-tail stock usually mounted in embossed silver. Surviving
examples are usually fitted with an imported flintlock. The silver
mounts are sometimes embossed with a combination of Turkish floral
decoration and motifs taken from European heraldry.

Perhaps because of predominating Western influences in the 18th
century, pistols were far more widely used in the Turkish Empire than
in Turkey itself. Blunderbusses were popular in the 18th and 19th
centuries as well as the type of pistol known to collectors as a 'Balkan'.
These include the rat-tail stock type of pistol described above, usually

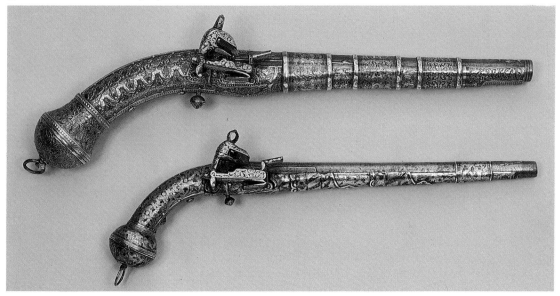

8

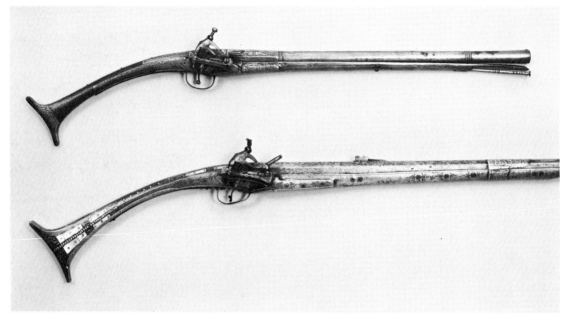

9

fitted with an imported flintlock and mounted in silver; and a more Western-looking pistol with an oval butt, also mounted in embossed silver and fitted with an imported flintlock. The stock decoration of this latter type is generally more restrained, consisting of flowers and trophies. The butts are often worked in a twisted design. Many of these are fitted with English locks.

The Caucasus

Firearms from the Caucasus are not only individual in their shape but also in their decoration. The main influences come from Persia and the main centre of production seems to have been around the village of Kubachi in Daghestan, an area which had a reputation for fine metal-work going back to medieval times. As with other Islamic areas the miquelet lock was the most favoured. Guns are usually fitted with straight stocks of oval section with a distinctive step behind the breech. The barrels are usually of watered steel imported from Persia, held to the stocks by capucines. The craftsmen of Kubachi in the Caucasus were celebrated for their use of silver-gilt inlaid with niello and also for the use of a heavy gold floral overlay against a background of blued steel. As with certain Turkish guns, the stocks of Caucasian guns are fitted with a substantial ivory block, forming the butt; this in turn is covered by applied silver-gilt plates inlaid with niello; the guns in plain state seem to have been delivered to craftsmen specialising in these silver and niello mounts, who then decorated the piece. Miquelet pistols from this area have downward curving stocks terminating in substantial ball butts, sometimes of ivory but often of wood. The stocks are overlaid with silver-gilt sheet, embossed and inlaid with niello in a design involving trilobed palmettes and flowers. Sometimes

9
a Miquelet carbine
The wooden stock mounted in engraved iron and brass, the barrel chiselled and engraved
Albanian, about 1800
78 cm   972-1884

b
Miquelet gun
The stock mounted in chiselled steel with engraved brass and mother o'pearl, the barrel inscribed 'Lazari Cominaz'
Albanian, about 1800
173 cm   1392-1903

10

bands of blued steel or nielloed silver were set into the stock and then overlaid with foliage and scrolling palmettes in relief. The effect is of considerable richness. The main centres of production of firearms from the 18th century onwards were the villages of Kubachi, Kumukh and Kazanistchi[7].

Persia

The matchlock gun seems to have been introduced to Persia some time in the 16th century possibly through trade with India. Long guns of light construction fitted with matchlocks are depicted in manuscripts of the late 16th and early 17th centuries. These have long full stocks of square section angled slightly at the breech with a substantial step behind the breech. The inspiration for the general shape seems to have come from Turkey but the narrow proportions and considerable length made Persian guns appear far more elegant. Persian gunmakers were quick to adopt the miquelet lock in the 17th century and continued to use this form of ignition until the 19th century. Persian gunsmiths were specially celebrated for the manufacture of watered steel

7. Chirkov D., *Daghestan Decorative Art*, p. 128 Moscow 1971

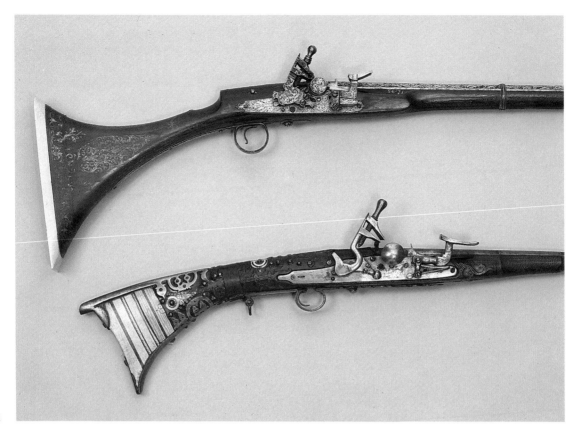

barrels which were widely traded in the East. These were long and, in contrast to Turkish examples, of comparatively light construction. Surviving barrels from the 17th and 18th centuries indicate that both octagonal and round types were fashionable. Straight, deep rifling is often found, and most have a substantial flange welded to the side of the breech containing a shallow circular pan. Both damascening and chiselling were used to decorate barrels. Examples from the 18th century have lines of interwoven scrolled palmettes in gold along the top of the barrel whilst the fashion for chiselled steel that prevailed in Persia in the late 18th and 19th centuries is reflected in barrels whose entire surfaces are chiselled with designs based on contemporary textiles. Persian calligraphers were especially skilful at engraving into metal. The maker's signature or owner's name and titles are usually beautifully engraved into the top of the barrel. Barrels were attached to the stock by means of capucines, often of precious metal. The stocks themselves were inlaid with stained ivory or characteristic mosaic work. Locks were damascened in silver or gold and on some especially fine guns mounts of enamelled gold are found.

A Persian form of blunderbuss, the 'Tapancha', was made in the latter part of the 18th century. Surviving examples have distinctive pierced silver mounts attached to ivory stocks and the locks are damascened in gold. Persian gunsmiths also made a form of short carbine, a

11
a Snaphance gun
The stock mounted in ivory and set with silver wire, the lock and barrel overlaid with gold
North African, about 1800
156.6 cm   56-1871

b Snaphance gun
The stock set with ivory plaques, silver mounts and pierced brass, the barrel with forged English proof marks
North African, about 1800
160 cm   1391-1903

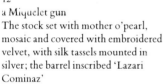

12

a Miquelet gun
The stock set with mother o'pearl,
mosaic and covered with embroidered
velvet, with silk tassels mounted in
silver; the barrel inscribed 'Lazari
Cominaz'
The stock bears the owner's name
'Hasan Aqa' and the name of the
maker 'Sayid Muhammad'
Turkish, late 17th century
167 cm   976-1884

b Miquelet gun
The stock set with ivory and overlaid
with mounts of pierced and engraved
silver; the barrel engraved with
panels, the lock set with panels of
engraved silver and brass. The lock is
of the Kabyle type, with a dog-lock.
Possibly made as a present for a
Kabyle chief
North African, about 1800
188 cm   M.47-1946

reduced version of their longer rifles. These are usually fitted with ball
triggers. One distinctive group of Persian pistols have wooden stocks
entirely covered by mosaic work. These appear to be comparatively
late as surviving examples are fitted with flintlocks and percussion
locks. It is very difficult to separate indigenous Persian gunsmiths'
work from that of India and the Caucasus as the same types of firearms
were widely used. Moreover a gun may have been made in one area
then decorated elsewhere to a particular client's taste. There is no
doubt that many so-called Indian guns are in fact Persian and that
many Persian firearms were probably made in the area of the Caucasus, then decorated in local Persian workshops.

Egypt

With the conquest of Egypt in the early 16th century by Selim the
Grim, Turkish influence became pre-eminent in this area. Very few
North African firearms dating from before the 18th century have been
identified but it is likely that in the 16th and 17th centuries these were
virtually identical to Turkish examples. The Arab gun used in the area
in the 18th century was very long, about 180cm and had a distinctive
fish-tail stock. The barrel was held to the stock by a series of capucines
made from brass, silver or occasionally wire. The stocks were of wood
with an ivory butt, the surface being inlaid with stained bone mosaic

or more rarely overlaid with silver sheet. In the late 18th and 19th centuries silver wire was sometimes let into the stock, scrolls and simple flowers being favourite motifs. Ball triggers were used but the most interesting feature was the lock. By the end of the 16th century Arab gunmakers had developed their own version of the miquelet lock, known as the 'Kabyle' lock. Operating in a similar manner to the miquelet, the Kabyle lock has a prominent safety catch operating on the back of the cock. The jaws are very long and the top jaw screw is fitted with two outward curving bars to allow the cock to be pulled back against the strong spring. These Kabyle locks are often set with brass inlays and decorated with engraving. They were especially popular in Tunisia and Algeria.

Maghreb
The Maghreb had considerable trade with Holland and England in the late 16th century and as a result a lock based on the Northern European snaphance was adopted by the local gunmakers for use on the long Arab gun. The lock had a laterally operating sear, pan cover and steel made as separate elements and an internal mainspring. These locks are often very plain but are somewhat large and more massively constructed than their Western counterparts. The standard gun of the Maghreb was very long; the capucines holding the barrel to the stock being formed as simple round bands with as many as twenty-five being used on some guns. The barrel was usually imported and the stock was flat with a profile resembling Northern European guns. The stock is mounted in brass or steel set with crudely engraved bone or ivory plaques and overlaid with silver bands. The use of coloured composition in the stock, usually red, is often found. Guns of this type were still being made and sold in the bazaars of Marrakesh this century. The English explorer Fawcett equipped himself with one when on a spying mission to Morocco before the First World War.[8]

Most of the pistols used in the region were either made up from imported elements, English locks and barrels being especially popular, or were imported as complete pieces then decorated locally. It has been pointed out[9] that a group of firearms including pistols with stocks

8. Now in the collection of the Royal Geographical Society, London
9. Blair C., *Pistols of the World*, p. 159, London 1958

13
Matchlock gun
The plain stock mounted with an elaborately chiselled barrel, probably of Indian origin
Central Asia? 18/19th century
113 cm   588-1876

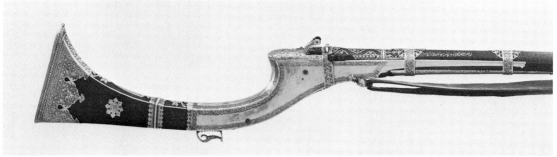

14
Matchlock gun (jezail)
The watered steel barrel overlaid with
gold, the stock mounted in engraved
gold. A sporting gun presented by the
Rajah of Jodhpur
Indian 18th century
143 cm   8571-1851

decorated with coral dating from about 1800, were almost certainly produced in Algiers.

There were considerable regional differences in the shape and decoration of gun stocks. Those from the Souss region of the Atlas have butts with a downward curve resembling Sardinian and Northern European stocks, whereas those from the North of the region have the standard fish-tail form. Guns from the region of the Sahara are inlaid with bone or ivory whereas those from the Tafraoute area of the Atlas have metal overlays and are set with silver studs.

Central Asia

Little information is available about the firearms used in Central Asia. A very crudely made form of matchlock gun can be attributed to this region. The stock is of plain wood, a tricker matchlock operates through a slot in the base of the stock and the barrel is held by plain brass capucines. The barrel, almost certainly an Indian import, is chiselled with a series of flutes laid out in a chevron pattern. The barrel is inlaid near the breech and at the muzzle with groups of brass studs, the muzzle being cut in a series of mouldings. The profile of the stock is that of the well-known Afghan 'Jezail' of which more below.

India

Firearms seem to have been introduced to India in the 15th century but it was during the Mogul period (1526-1857) that they were most widely used. Under Akbar (1556-1605) firearms were used both for sport and war. Most of the surviving firearms date from after the 17th century. Matchlocks were especially favoured throughout the period and continued to be manufactured long after the introduction of the flintlock. The main types of firearms include the 'Toradar', a long gun with square or polygonal stock, guns with so called Afghan stocks called 'Jezails', the stock curving sharply downwards and terminating in a wide flat butt, and a form made in Mysore with a flat hook-shaped butt. The barrels are finely chiselled and damascened with gold and silver, the stocks inlaid with ivory and metal. The stock below the breech is usually completely sheathed in steel or brass, often decorated with engraving or damascening.

Accessories

The operation of a firearm requires a large number of accessories. These include a ramrod, powder flask, a container for bullet or cartridge, a set of tools to dismantle the lock, a priming flask and powder tester. Islamic gunmakers used great ingenuity in the manufacture of these necessary accoutrements, and there was considerable regional variation in their shape and decoration. Turkish powder flasks were made in a variety of materials and shapes. These include a small lightly curved type fitted with a spring cap attached to the top with rings to allow it to be suspended from the belt. These were made not only from horn or wood but also in steel and brass. Some luxurious versions were also made in silver mounted in coral. Persian flasks are usually of steel or brass, they follow the Turkish shape but are usually more finely worked. Persian gunsmiths specialised in the production of finely pierced and damascened steel flasks, and Persian craftsmen were very skilful at producing flasks of unusual shapes. Priming flasks of watered steel survive in the shape of fish and birds. The flasks of the Caucasus area were often of silver decorated with niello. One very exotic 18th-century flask is made from a sea-shell mounted in nielloed silver.

North African flasks were sometimes made in the form of a circular box of brass or steel with a long nozzle, with rings attached to the top. Mechanical devices for testing powder were also a favourite of the Islamic gunsmith. Turkish powder testers were made in silver mounted in coral and some Persian examples were made in steel and combined the functions of powder tester, measure and spanner in one tool.

A number of very exotic Indian powder flasks were made in the 17th and 18th centuries. Indian craftsmen were especially fond of the combination of wood and ivory. Some were made in the shape of a fish with an upcurving tail overlaid with engraved ivory plaques over the entire surface.

One accessory which seems to have survived in considerable numbers is the small box, usually made from brass, used by Turkish troops to carry ammunition. These were designed to be worn on the belt and have a closely fitting hinged lid. They are generally decorated

15
Accessories

a Powder-horn
Wood mounted in silver with niello,
the cap of ivory
Caucasus, 18th century
16.3 cm   63-1897

b Powder-horn
Chiselled steel inlaid with gold
Persian, 18th century
12.5 cm   272-1896

c Powder-horn
Silver with mounts of embossed
silver-gilt and coral, with suspension
chain and tassel
Turkish, 18th century
10.5 cm   754-1893

d Powder-measure
Silver, parcel-gilt with a graduated
slide, mounted with filigree and coral
Turkish, late 18th century
17.6 cm   755-1893

e Powder-flask
Shell mounted in silver with niello
Caucasus late 18th century
15.8 cm   354-1864

f Combination tool, incorporating a
powder-tester, spanner, and powder-
measure. Chiselled and engraved steel
Persian, 19th century
16.6 cm   M.825-1928

with coarse embossing. The majority that survive date from the late
18th or 19th centuries.

Another distinctively Turkish accoutrement is the steel ramrod
known as a 'Suma'. These were simply rods fitted with a substantial
suspension hook at the top, often made in cast silver used to ram home
the charge in the firearm. A type of combination tool was also used
widely in the East with firearms. It is shaped like a 'T' and is a combination of screw-driver, hammer and pricker to clean out the touch
hole. The most sophisticated examples of this tool known as
'Eslabones' were made in Spain and they are found in those areas of the
East mostly under Spanish influence and in North Africa.

Swords

The sword and the dagger are the weapons most associated with Islam and, as with certain other Islamic weapons, shapes and decorative treatments can be traced back to pre-Islamic times.

Turkey

A distinctive Turkish sword had already developed by the 10th century. This had a short broad straight blade, small pommel of spherical form and distinctive downward curving quillons curving towards the blade. A sword of this form is depicted on the well known 10th-century figure of Goliath from the Armenian church of 'Gagik' on Aght'amar, an island in Lake Van. The remains of an actual sword of this type were found in 1977 in an 11th-century shipwreck at Serce Liman, Turkey. Only the hilt and part of the blade survive. The hilt of cast bronze has quillons folded close to the sides of the blade; the grip is circular with raised mouldings and apparently made in one with the grip is a small cap-shaped pommel with fluted sides and a small ring attached to it. This type of hilt is clearly the ancestor of a group of straight bladed Turkish swords preserved in Topkapi and Askeri Museums in Istanbul. There are slight variations within the general group, but the bronze mounted grip and small cap pommel, with attached ring, are usually found. In some examples the quillons are straight with slightly curving terminals and are made of steel. These swords seem to date from the 14th or 15th centuries. Although many bear inscriptions relating to their deposition in the arsenal at Alexandria, it is tempting to suggest that they were an indigenous Turkish form, on the basis of the evidence suggested above. Further support for a Turkish origin for this form is the substantial number of later versions of this hilt form with recognisably Turkish decoration[10]. The form seems to have been used until the 18th century. One example with a simplified version of this hilt is decorated with enamel and is fitted with a fine quality European blade.

Collectors and students are more familiar with the traditional Turkish sword known as a 'Yataghan'. In its classic form this has a short

---

10. For another see Nicolle D., *Early Medieval Islamic Arms and Armour,* Fig. 119, Instituto de Estudios Sobre Armas Antiquas, 1976

16

16
Sword of Selim the Grim
Watered steel blade, the grip of carved ivory
Turkish, first quarter of 16th century
Topkapi Palace

17
Sword
Watered steel blade inlaid with gold, the mounts of silver inlaid with gold
Turkish, late 15th century
Topkapi Palace

17

hilt without a guard, with two prominent ears forming the pommel. The single edged blade is usually formed as a very elongated 'S' shape although examples with straight blade are certainly known. The basic hilt shape is pre-Islamic and hilts from Luristan dating from 1000 BC in bronze are almost identical in construction.

Various regional forms, especially from the Balkans, are known but these differences are of decoration rather than shape. Perhaps the finest surviving yataghan is that made for Suleyman II in Topkapi dated 1526, which has a beautifully chiselled blade overlaid with gold, the hilt being of carved ivory inlaid with gold. Some yataghans have horn or wood hilts and it is this type which is preserved in considerable quantities in the Army Museum in Vienna, said to have been taken at the Siege of Vienna in 1683. There seems to have been a vogue for particularly elaborate specimens in the late 18th and early 19th centuries. Some have scabbards and hilts of silver gilt heavily embossed and set with coral or have blades damascened in gold with poems or Koranic verses.

The date of the introduction of the curved sword to Islam is not yet clear. Curved single-edged swords are shown on frescoes from

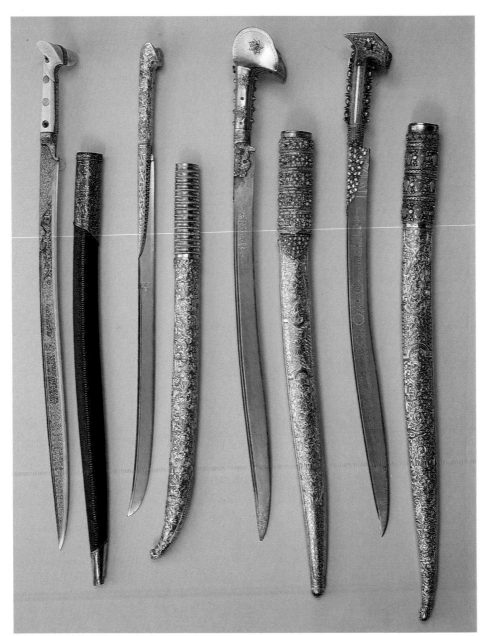

18
Turkish swords (yataghans)
a Steel mounts overlaid in gold, ivory
grip, the blade bearing pious
invocations and heroic verses, the
signature of the maker 'Umar' and the
name of an owner 'Muhamad Rasid
Pasha'
Dated 1840
73 cm   M.38-1973

b Grip and scabbard of embossed
silver, the blade inlaid in gold
Early 19th century
69.4 cm   892-1874

c Grip and scabbard of silver-gilt
decorated with filigree, the blade
inlaid in gold
c.1800
72.5 cm   895-1874

d Grip and scabbard of silver decorated with coral and filigree, the blade
inlaid in silver. Said to have been
acquired in Herzogoviňa
Dated 1797 AD
70.1 cm   M.964-1928

19

a Sword
The watered steel blade inlaid in gold,
the grip of carved jade, the quillons
cast silver, the scabbard of embossed
silver. The grip has been taken from
an Indian dagger
Turkish, 18th century
90.2 cm   M.46-1946

b Sword
The blade of watered steel overlaid
with gold with an inscription declar-
ing it to be Damascus work
Turkish, dated 1634/5
Length 86.0 cm   M.32-1965

c Sword and scabbard
The blade of watered steel, the hilt
and scabbard mounted in silver; the
blade inlaid with the name of the
maker 'Ustad Husayn'
Presented to General Browne-
Clayton after the battle of Alexandria
in 1801
Egyptian, about 1800, the blade
probably earlier
Length 89.0 cm   M.64-1934

d Sword and scabbard
The watered steel blade inlaid in gold
with verses, the hilt of blued steel
damascened in gold. The decoration
on the hilt and scabbard based upon
Western sources
Turkish, about 1850, the blade
probably earlier
96.5 cm   M.37-1973

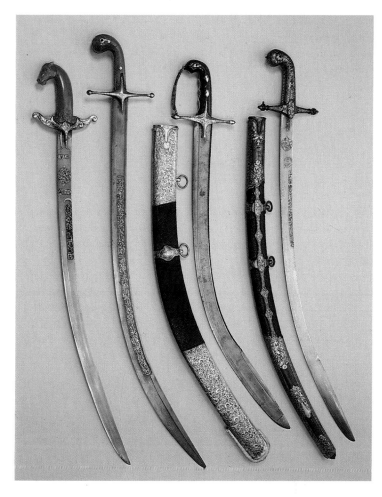

19

Turkestan as early as the 9th century AD. Preserved in the Topkapi
Palace are a series of slightly curved swords attributed to early Turkish
rulers. The dates of these are still controversial as some of the inscriptions are likely to be later additions. There are however some 15th-
century Turkish swords in Topkapi whose dates in the writer's view
can be accepted. These are fitted with straight and curved blades. The
straight blades are broad and double edged, the curved blades are also
very broad, often with a shallow channel, and a short section of the
back, near the point, is ground down to form a back edge. The guard
consists of a substantial cross with square or spatulate ends. The centre
of the guard extends down the blade and down the hilt presumably as a
reinforcement for the grip. The tang is either straight or more often
slightly curved. The pommel is usually a small metal cap covering the
end of the tang. By the 16th century the curvature of the blade had
increased and the pommel cap was set at a definite right angle to the
grip. This basic shape, with slight variations, remained in use until the
19th century. At some period in the latter part of the 16th century

blades were forged with a substantial flat back, and developed a graceful curve.

At some time in the 17th century there was a tendency for the pommel and grip to be made in one, usually of horn or wood. Grips were made of a variety of materials, horn, wood and precious metal were all used; some swords were mounted with Mogul jade hilts. Scabbards were of wood covered in leather; in the 18th- and 19th-centuries, they were often made entirely of silver embossed in late Ottoman taste. It was these late Ottoman swords that were adopted by French generals after the Egyptian campaign of 1801.

Arabia and North Africa

Early Arab swords preserved in Istanbul are straight and broad. However curved single edged swords were certainly in use in Egypt by the 13th century as is shown by their appearance on metalwork and in manuscripts. An inlaid figure on the base of a pen-box in the British Museum dated 1280 is holding a clearly defined curved sword, but there are earlier illustrations of such swords. The hilts of early Arab swords have rather slender long quillons terminating in spatulate ends. Very few of these early Arab swords have ever come onto the market.

The type of Arab sword most commonly found are those used in North Africa and the Maghreb. The classic sword of the area is the

21
Hilt of a sword
The grip of ivory inlaid with gold, the guard of silver-gilt and niello, the central panel of cast gold. The blade has been deliberately snapped off short, perhaps indicating that it was taken as loot for its precious metal
Turkish c.1650
20.5 cm   982–1884

20

20
Portrait of Tobias Blosse
This captain of a Trained Band is shown wearing a typical Moroccan sword and holding a staff of office. These swords with their distinctive hilts seem to have been fashionable in the 17th century in England, as they are shown in other portraits of the period
English School, about 1617
Ipswich Museum and Art Gallery

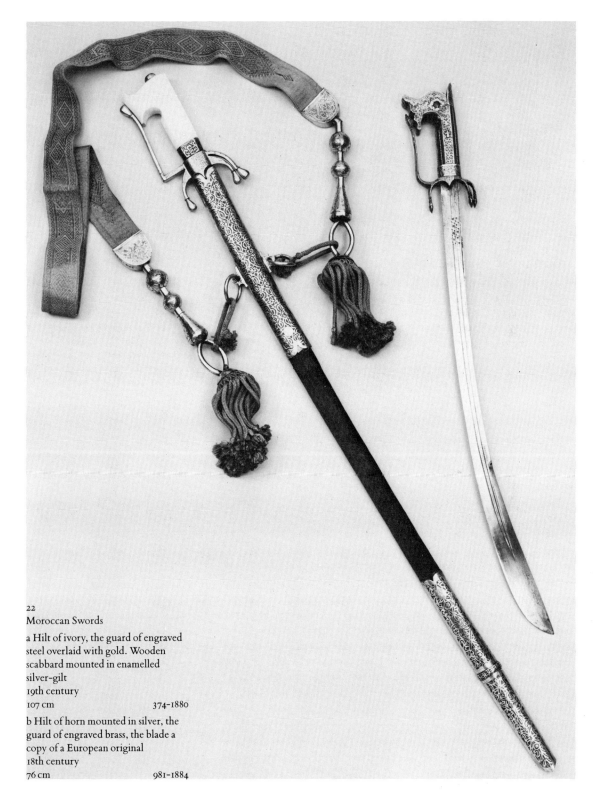

22
Moroccan Swords

a Hilt of ivory, the guard of engraved
steel overlaid with gold. Wooden
scabbard mounted in enamelled
silver-gilt
19th century
107 cm   374-1880

b Hilt of horn mounted in silver, the
guard of engraved brass, the blade a
copy of a European original
18th century
76 cm   981-1884

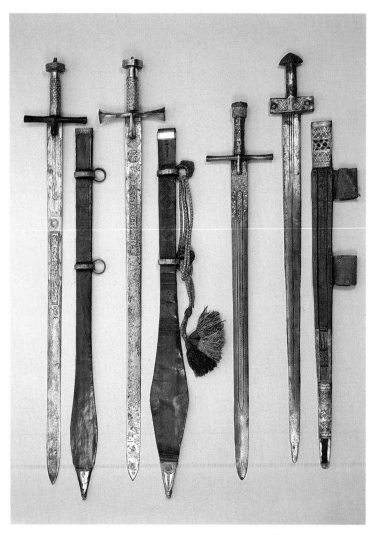

23

23
Swords from North Africa
a The hilt mounted in silver, the blade
etched with designs based on German
imported blades
Sudanese, 19th century
106 cm
Private collection

b The hilt mounted in silver, the grip
of gold. This is one of the heirloom
blades owned by Sultan Ali Dinar,
killed in 1916
Sudanese (Darfur), late 18th century
with later mounts
102 cm
Private collection

c The hilt mounted in silver, the blade
damascened in gold with inscriptions
and the maker's name Abdallah Bin
Ibrahim Sudanese, the hilt 19th
century, the blade early 17th century
85 cm   M.47-1953

d The hilt of engraved brass with
traces of tinning, the scabbard
mounted in pierced brass fitted with
an imported German blade
North African (Southern Sahara),
18th century
97 cm   1154-1903

'Nimcha'. This has more than a hint of European influence especially
in the form of the hilt, which is fitted with a knuckle bow linked to
curved quillons. These hilts are found mounted with straight and
curved blades, the straight blades were usually imported from Europe.
This type of sword continued in use until the 19th century. The Arab
version survived in its straight form in North Africa and the Sudan
until this century in the form of the Sudanese sword known as a
'Kaskara'. The straight quillons and blade differ only slightly from
their 13th- and 14th-century Arab forebears. Most of the straight
blades were imported, but there are examples of locally made blades,
found with these hilts. Early Turkish hilt forms also survived in the
Maghreb. The swords used by the Tuaregs and warriors of the Sahara
had hilts which were very similar to the early bronze mounted hilts of
medieval Turkey. As with the Sudanese swords, the majority of the
blades were imported from the West.

24 (opposite)
Sword, and scabbard
The blade of watered steel, the
mounts of steel inlaid with gold.
Inlaid in gold on each side of the blade
are verses and Koranic inscriptions.
On the back edge is inlaid a genealogy
of Shah Tamasp (1524-76). The blade
has been shortened and the profile
altered at some period. Presented to
the Indian Office in 1855 by a Colonel
Pennington and said to have come
from Lahore. The scabbard is later but
the steel mounts inlaid with gold are
contemporary with the hilt
Persian, about 1530
108 cm   I.S.-3378

25   25

a Sword and scabbard
The hilt and scabbard-mounts of gold set with pearls and
precious stones. Presented to Lord Athlone by King Ibn-Saud
in 1928
The blade Persian 17th century, the hilt and scabbard Saudi-
Arabian
19/20th century   M.293-1976

b Sword and scabbard
Hilt and scabbard mounts of gold. Presented to Lord Athlone
by Sheik Iza of Bahrain in 1928
The blade Persian, 18th century, the hilt and scabbard Saudi-
Arabian,
19/20th century   M.294-1976

24

The swords associated with Saudi Arabia are distinguished by their lavish gold and silver mounts. Imported Persian blades, some of considerable age, were mounted in gold. The quillons are usually of iron plated with silver, the hilt and scabbard mounts of stamped gold. Grips are of ivory mounted in gold and the pommel cap is set at right angles to the grip. The pommel caps on Saudi swords are very long and are usually linked by a double chain to the back of the quillons.

Persia

The swords illustrated in the early Persian manuscripts can be compared with surviving examples preserved in Topkapi. A miniature from the Demotte Shah-Name of *c.* 1340 shows curved swords with flat spatulate quillons, straight grip and flat pommel cap. A similar hilt is fitted to a broad two edged straight blade in the Topkapi collection which presumably dates from the same period or earlier. Some 14th- and 15th-century Persian swords have quillons with terminals chiselled as dragons' heads. The quillons turn at an angle towards the blade and perhaps the finest specimen in Topkapi of this type has the grip and quillons of carved jade. By the 16th century, Persian swords were fitted with a broad curved single edged blade usually of watered steel, with short quillons terminating in round knobs. Blades sometimes are chiselled with shallow channels running along their length.

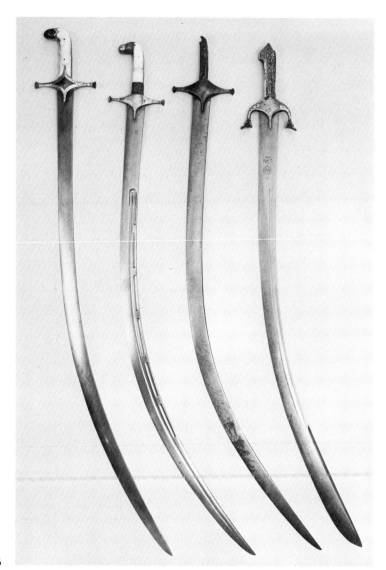

26

a Sword
The watered steel blade showing the
pattern known as 'Muhammad's
ladder', the hilt overlaid with gold
Persian 17th century. The later
mounts probably Indian
102 cm
Private collection

b Sword
The blade of watered steel damascened in gold with inscriptions giving
the name of Shah Safi (1629-42)
Persian 17th century
100 cm   I.S.3375

c Sword
The watered steel blade showing the
pattern known as 'Muhammad's
ladder'
Persian, 17th century
99.5 cm   M.10-1958

d Sword
The blade of watered steel, the hilt
chiselled and overlaid with gold. The
blade inlaid with the name of the
swordsmith 'Kalb Ali'
Persian, late 17th century
95.5 cm   614-1876

This basic shape was retained until the 19th century. The dating of
Persian blades without the assistance of inscriptions is very difficult. In
general, the very broad heavy blades with slight curvature are likely to
date from the 16th to 17th century period. Persian blades of later date
tended to be both lighter and shorter. Several examples of these light,
short blades bearing the names of 18th-century owners are recorded.
Older blades often show signs of alteration and re-mounting such as
old rivet holes in the tang.

Owners, if they are well known, are usually datable and genealo-
gies are sometimes inlaid in gold into the blade. The name of a maker
such as Asad-Allah of Isphahan whose name appears on many Persian
blades is no guarantee of antiquity. This maker is supposed to have
worked in the 17th century but his name appears on blades that are

27

27
Sword (*opposite*)
The hilt of carved jade mounted in
gold, the blade of watered steel
Persian, late 15th century
Topkapi Palace, Istanbul

28
Engraved 'signature' on a Persian
sword-blade, that of the swordsmith
Kalb Ali. This name is found on
swords of various dates, and may have
been intended as mark of quality,
rather than the name of an individual
maker

29
Figure of a horseman
Carrying a bow and wearing a sword.
From a large circular dial of gilt and
engraved copper
Persian, late 16th century   1577-1904

demonstrably later. The name seems to have been put on blades as a
'brand' name rather than an indication of the manufacturer. The hilts
of later Persian blades are very fragile and the two thin bone or ivory
plaques which form the grip must have been easily shattered when
used to strike a blow. Most of these are reinforced with wire and must
have been replaced many times during the life of a blade. Scabbards are
usually of wood covered in stamped leather with steel or precious
metal mounts. Persian blades were very highly prized and were
exported throughout the Islamic world.

Spain
Only a few of the swords made in Moorish Spain have survived and
these are hardly representative as they are nearly all made for kings.
Their straight bladed swords are splendidly mounted in enamelled
gold. Humbler versions must have been made from the evidence of a
single scabbard chape of gilt copper, from one of these swords. This
dates from the end of the 15th century, the last period of an Islamic
presence in Spain.

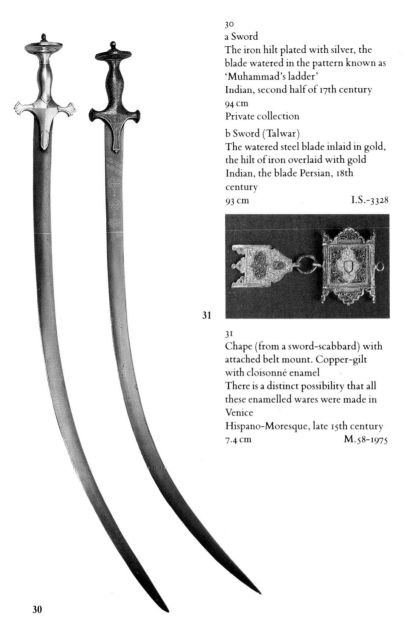

30

30
a Sword
The iron hilt plated with silver, the
blade watered in the pattern known as
'Muhammad's ladder'
Indian, second half of 17th century
94 cm
Private collection

b Sword (Talwar)
The watered steel blade inlaid in gold,
the hilt of iron overlaid with gold
Indian, the blade Persian, 18th
century
93 cm   I.S.-3328

31

31
Chape (from a sword-scabbard) with
attached belt mount. Copper-gilt
with cloisonné enamel
There is a distinct possibility that all
these enamelled wares were made in
Venice
Hispano-Moresque, late 15th century
7.4 cm   M.58-1975

32
Sword
The hilt of blued steel overlaid with
gold, the watered steel blade treated
with acid to produce a chevron
pattern
Indian (Rajasthan), early 19th century
I.S.87-1981

32

India

The development of the sword in India merits a book in its own right.
There is space here only to discuss the most important hilt form. In the
Islamic period, probably in the later part of the 16th century, a form of
sword known as the 'talwar' was adopted. This had a single edged
curved blade and a hilt of Persian form with straight quillons, grip
formed of two plates of wood or ivory pinned through the tang and a
pommel cap set at right angles to the hilt. By the 17th century a form of

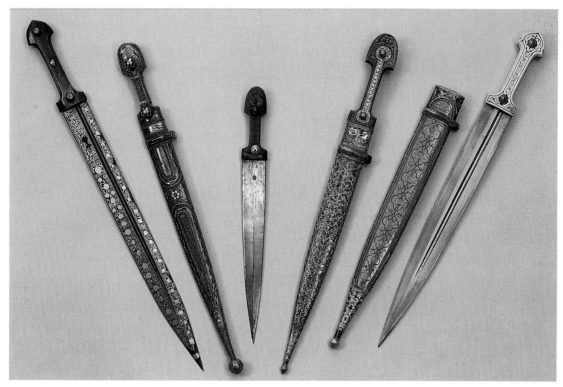

33
Daggers from the Caucasus (Kindjal)

a Horn hilt mounted in steel inlaid
with gold
Early 19th century
55 cm   740-1889

b Mounts of silver with niello
? Date
46 cm   377-1924

c Horn hilt mounted in silver-gilt and
niello
Dated 1866 A.D.
36.5 cm   M.1061-1910

d Horn hilt inlaid with gold, sheath of
openwork silver-gilt and niello,
enclosing a panel of blued steel overlaid with gold. Fitted with a by-knife
at the back of the scabbard
Early 19th century
48 cm   620-1894

e Ivory hilt inlaid with gold, the
sheath of silver-gilt and niello enclosing a panel of tinted ivory
From the Daghestan region, dated
1861 AD
50.6 cm   619-1894

hilt had developed which became the standard Indian type. This had a round concave saucer-shaped pommel, bulbous grip and straight quillons terminating in large knobs. The centre of the guard projected down the blade at either side. This hilt was a combination of earlier Indian forms with influences from Persia and was used with slight variations until this century. The evidence from manuscript illustrations suggests that the hilts with deeply concave pommels and flat quillons are from the 16th–17th century. A flat pommel, and round quillons usually indicates a late date, that is to say from the 18th or 19th centuries.

The Caucasus

The best known edged weapon of the Caucasus region, was a type of short sword known as a 'Kindjal'. This had a broad two-edged straight blade tapering to form a long point, set in a hilt without a guard, with a square sectioned grip and rounded flat pommel. The design closely resembles the Roman 'gladius' and it is tempting to suggest that this was its ancestor. The majority of swords of this form date from the 18th or early 19th century and were made by Amuzgi and Kharbuk armourers then decorated by the craftsmen of Kubachi and the surrounding area. In the 19th century these craftsmen also produced some fine versions of the traditional Cossack sword known as the 'shaska'. Many of these were decorated to the taste of Russian officers who wore the sword as part of military dress.

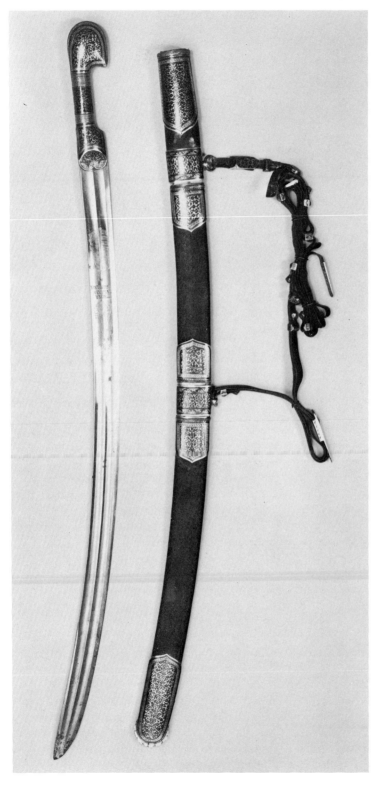

34

34
Sword
'Shasqa', the blade engraved with
Latin mottos, the hilt of silver set with
niello
Caucasus, about 1850
95.3 cm   694–1889

Daggers

Islamic daggers show a large number of regional variations in their construction and ornament, and considerations of space will only allow here a discussion of the main types. Both curved and straight blades are found on Eastern daggers and in many instances blades manufactured in one region have been mounted in hilts made elsewhere. The problems of trying to establish the date and provenance of a particular item are therefore very difficult.

A group of 15th- and 16th-century Persian daggers have however been recognised recently. Characteristics include straight or slightly curved blades decorated with chiselling. Inlaid in gold into the surface of the blade are verses from poems.

Most collections of Eastern weapons include examples of the Persian short dagger known as a 'Kard'. The blades are usually of watered steel, the grip being formed of two plaques of bone or morse ivory held by rivets. The more elaborate of these daggers have finely chiselled scrolls and arabesques on the blade near the grip, the blade being straight and single edged with a flat back. A number are inscribed with the makers' names and dates. The majority of the dated examples were made around 1800.

Non-specialists generally think of Eastern daggers as all being sharply curved. In fact only certain types of dagger have this feature. They include the well-known 'Jambiyas' of Arabia, usually mounted in gold or silver. The blades are normally broad and double edged with a prominent central rib. They are usually lightly curved whereas the scabbards form a 'U' shape curving upwards towards the hand. As well-known are the curved daggers of the Atlas and Sahara regions of North Africa. These have distinctive grips formed of wood or horn mounted in engraved brass and silver. It is only possible to establish the exact locality where these daggers were made by analysing the decoration on the hilt and scabbard.

Another characteristic of Islamic daggers is the widespread use of various types of hardstone to form the hilt. These range from carved rock crystal, jade of every colour and design, to various types of agate. The shape of sword-hilts had an obvious influence on the design of these hardstone hilts.

Many of the Mogul jade hilts for daggers are carved so that the

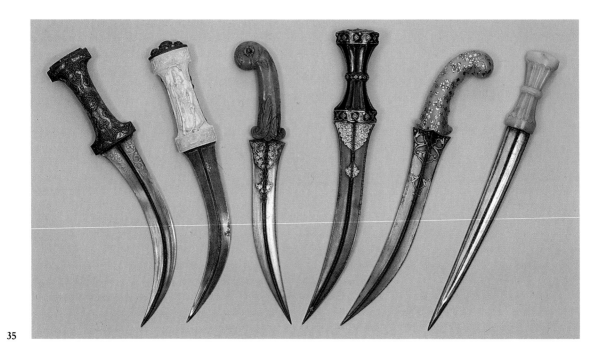

pommel projects at an angle from the grip imitating the angular
mounts found on sword hilts. Jade hilts were carved in a variety of
designs; horses' heads, flowers and occasionally human figures. The
jade hilts of Mogul India were frequently set with gems or inlaid with
gold or silver. One form of jade hilt which is variously attributed both
to Turkish and Indian workshops has a distinctive 'waisted' profile
carved with a series of shallow flutes, the central section of the grip
carved as a narrow raised band.

In the late 18th- and 19th-century Persian craftsmen produced some
fine carved daggers, the hilts of which were of ivory or bone, sometimes being set with stones at the pommel. Floral ornament and
figurative designs form the normal decorative repertoire. These often
bear makers' names and dates. During the 19th century there was a
revival in Persia of styles that had been fashionable in the 15th and 16th
centuries. Under this influence some very fine steel-hilted daggers
were produced in the first half of that century. The hilts are of watered
steel chiselled with calligraphy and overlaid with gold.

Some very fine steel-hilted daggers were also made in India,
especially during the 16th and 17th centuries. The hilts and blades were
made from watered steel forged as one complete element, often with a
knuckle-guard extending either from the quillons or from the 'T'
shaped pommel.

Horn, ivory and bone were used extensively in Islamic lands to
make the grips for daggers. Some very fine dagger handles of ivory
carved with interlaced arabesques were produced in the 16th century
by the craftsmen of Ottoman Turkey.

35
Daggers

a Watered steel, chiselled and overlaid
with gold
Persian, 18/19th century
35.5 cm   577-1876

b Watered steel blade inlaid in gold,
the hilt of carved ivory set with stones
Persian, dated 1838
35.3 cm   717-1889

c Watered steel blade inlaid in gold,
the hilt and scabbard mounts of
Mughal jade
Indian, late 17th century
40.3 cm   721-1889

d Watered steel blade inlaid in gold,
grip of carved black jade set with
rubies mounted in gold
Persian, 17th century
38 cm   722-1889

e Watered steel blade chiselled and
inlaid with gold, the grip of jade
inlaid with gold
Persian, 17th century
39.1 cm   719-1889

f Watered steel mounted in jade
Turkish, 17th century
38.2 cm   814-1893

36
Daggers from North Africa

a Horn hilt mounted in silver
19th century
40 cm   4-1898

b Wooden hilt mounted in enamelled
silver and engraved brass
From the Tafraoute region in the
Atlas, 19th century
40.2 cm   M.644-1911

As with some Islamic sword types, certain hilt forms found with daggers can be traced back to the bronze daggers used in Luristan in pre-Islamic times. The well-known hilt-form with twin discs at the pommel – the so called 'ear' daggers – is an example of such a survival. First used in Luristan, then in modified form in Moorish Spain, it was quite extensively adopted in the West during the 15th and 16th centuries. The author has also seen a series of Indian daggers of traditional design bearing dates from the 1930s. These were presumably made as presents but in appearance and material they hardly differed from examples normally dated to the 17th and 18th centuries.

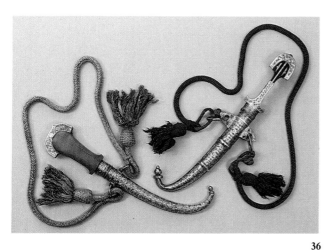

36

37
Persian daggers

a Watered steel, chiselled and inlaid with gold, the blade inlaid
with the name of the maker 'Ali Akbar'
Late 18th century
38.8 cm   824-1893

b Watered steel chiselled and inlaid with gold
Late 18th century
40 cm   Circ.292-1921

c Watered steel overlaid with engraved gold, the blade inlaid
with engraved, gold, and with the maker's name 'Muhammad
Hadi'
Late 18th century
35.2 cm   712-1889

d Watered steel, overlaid with gold, the blade inlaid with the
maker's name
Late 18th century
33.6 cm   715-1889

e Watered steel, inlaid with gold, the grip of horn, the blade
inlaid with the maker's name 'Ghulamali'
Dated 1806-7
31 cm   M.72-1934

f Watered steel, overlaid with gold, the grip of watered steel
overlaid with gold
About 1800
30.5 cm   568-1876

g Watered steel overlaid with gold, the sheath of pierced and
engraved silver set with stones and niello
About 1800
35.8 cm   1225-1888

37

39

Maces, axes and staff-weapons

The mace in Islamic lands, like its Western counterpart, had two roles, as a symbol of office carried by a military leader, and as a weapon. Its shape was to a very great extent established in pre-Islamic times. Mace-heads cast in bronze by the craftsmen of Luristan in Persia around the eighth century BC exhibit many of the features to be seen on later examples. These include the use of a series of flanges arranged around a central block, and the use of raised square studs.

Very few medieval maces from Islam have been published or recognised. However, there are manuscript illustrations of the early 14th century which depict mace-heads and a very small number of bronze examples, often misdescribed, of the 13th and 14th centuries have survived. A warrior is shown in an early 14th-century Persian manuscript wielding a mace with a head formed of a series of straight flanges set around a substantial cylindrical block. The handle, presumably of wood, is comparatively long[11]. Another mace-head is made of cast bronze inlaid with silver. The head is faceted and shaped rather like a flask; it is fitted with a substantial hook at one side[12]. This example is Persian and dates from the 13th or 14th century. Another type, also of cast bronze, is shaped like a long bottle with rounded top, which has also been dated to the 14th century.

Preserved in the armoury at Topkapi in Istanbul are a series of steel maces. These are of various shapes and include examples with bulbous heads, maces set with a series of radiating flanges, and one in which the head is formed as a lion standing squarely on a substantial base. This last must have been intended for symbolic use only. The shafts of these maces are also made of steel and are decorated with chiselling. They have been attributed to the Mameluks and if this attribution is correct, then they are likely to be part of the spoils taken by the Ottoman Sultan Selim the Grim in his successful Egyptian campaign in the early part of the 16th century.

The mace with a head formed of flanges was widely used in Islam. In Turkey the head is often set with a large number of flanges, put

11. See E. Kuhnel, *Islamic Arts*, p. 44, Brunswick 1963
12. See G. Fehervari, *Islamic Metalwork*, plate 50, London 1976

38

38
Mace
The cartouche on the back of this steel mace shows the signature of the maker 'Haji Abbas', a Persian who specialized in chiselled steel, and is supposed to have worked in the 17th century. However, the majority of the objects bearing this signature, including this mace, date from the 19th century

697-1889

39

a Mace
Watered steel, chiselled and overlaid
with gold. Signed 'Faiz Allah'
Persian, first quarter of the 18th
century
65 cm   742-1889

b Mace
in the form of a demon's head;
watered steel, chiselled, etched and
overlaid with gold. Signed on the
back 'Haji Abbas'
Persian 19th century
89.5 cm   67-1889

c Double-bladed parade axe
Watered steel, chisselled and overlaid
with gold, the shaft overlaid with
silver
Persian 18/19th century
94.6 cm   487-1874

d Axe
Chiselled steel with brass mounts
Indo-Persian, 18/19th century
82.3 cm   681-1889

e Mace of office
Jade mounted in nielloed silver,
inscribed with the owner's name
'Mehmet Neshat Effendi', an officer
of police
Turkish, 18th century
59.3 cm   M.20-1965

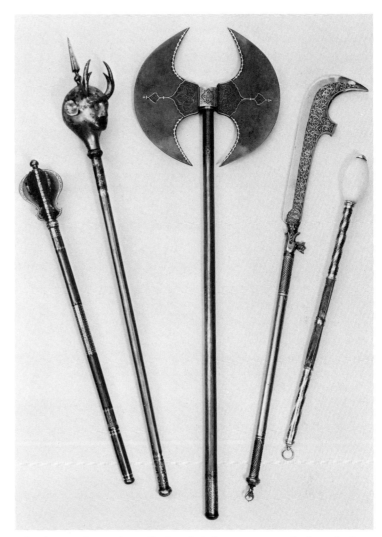

closely together and usually fitted with a comparatively short shaft. In Persia a larger, more elegant mace was carried. This had few flanges and a long shaft with a knob at the end to prevent the shaft slipping from the hand. The flanges present an 'S' shaped profile and both shaft and head are sometimes damascened in gold. It has not escaped the notice of arms and armour specialists that the flanged mace of Islam was the direct ancestor of the elegant European Gothic maces – so much admired by collectors.

In Turkey, the mace was used in war until comparatively late. A number of steel war-maces, as well as the highly decorative commanders' maces, were captured by European forces in the wars against the Turks during the 17th century. Maces of Turkish form were also carried extensively by the troops of Poland and Hungary during the period. Most of these were purely for ceremonial use as symbols of command, and were made in precious metal or gilt copper and brass.

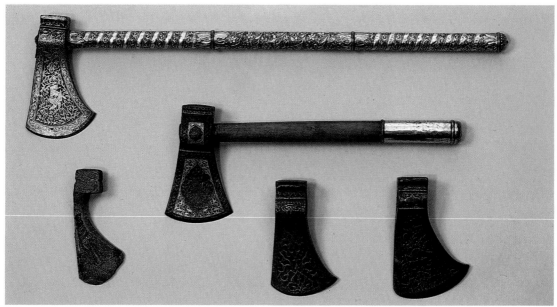

40
Saddle-Axes

a Chiselled steel inlaid with gold
Inscribed as having been made at Lahore, and bearing the spurious signature of the craftsman Lotf'Ali
Hindustan, 19th century
14.1 cm   III-1888

b Bronze, plated with silver and engraved with scrolls
Syrian 12/13th century
13,2 cm   M.145-1919

c Chiselled steel, blued and inlaid with gold
With the signature of the craftsman Lotf'Ali Gholam
Persian, c.1735

d Chiselled steel
Persian, first half of the 17th century
13.1 cm   1737-1912

e Chiselled steel
Persian, first half of the 18th century
13.7 cm   M.461-1910

41
a Javelins and case
Wood, with heads of steel inlaid with gold, the case of velvet covered wood, mounted in silver (the flights are missing)
Indo-Persian, 18th century
80 cm   979-1884

b Javelin
Chiselled steel overlaid with gold
Persian, 18/19th century
86 cm   600-1875

c Javelin
Chiselled steel overlaid with gold
Persian, 18th century
77 cm   603-1876

Eastern European types can often be distinguished by the use of applied shagreen to the shaft, which in general is made from wood with metal mounts.

Many collections of Islamic arms contain maces with heads in the form of bulls or demons, usually of watered steel damascened in gold. A bull-headed mace is said to have been carried by Genghiz Khan and Tamerlane. These are also depicted in the hands of well-known characters from Persian legend, inlaid into metal vessels and illustrated in manuscripts of the medieval period. The majority of these figurative maces found in collections date from the 18th or 19th centuries.

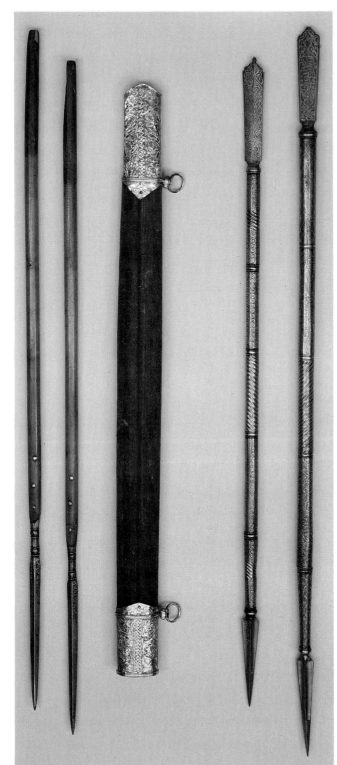

42
a Lance-head with twin blades
Watered steel, chiselled and overlaid
with gold
Persian, 17/18th century
27.7 cm   726-1889

b Lance-head
Watered steel, chiselled and overlaid
with gold
Persian, 19th century
52.5 cm   704-1889

c Lance-head
Watered steel, chiselled and overlaid
with gold
Persian, 18th century
47.6 cm   708-1889

d Lance-head with twin blades
Watered steel, the blades inlaid with
brass, the socket overlaid with gold
Persian, 18/19th century
60.7 cm   729-1889

e Lance-head
Chiselled steel overlaid with gold
Indo-Persian, 19th century
38.3 cm   727-1889

They appear to have been made solely for parade.

Collectors and students will encounter a type of mace with an oval head carved from onyx, marble or some other stone. These are usually fitted with silver shafts and mounts. Most appear to be of Turkish origin as some are inscribed with Turkish names and titles, but it has recently been shown that similar stone-headed maces were used in Bokhara in the 19th century. The inscriptions on some Turkish versions indicate that they were carried as symbols of authority by the officers of specialist troops.

The axe, like the mace, has its origins in pre-Islamic times. The small bronze axe-heads of Luristan are well known. Small hand axes with blades of crescent form are known from the 12th and 13th centuries, as illustrations in manuscripts and decoration on vessels. Also depicted are very large two-handed axes which from their context were intended for parade use even in these early sources. They were usually carried as a symbol of rank before commanders or religious leaders.

Some Mameluk axes of the 14th and 15th centuries are preserved in Topkapi. These have large crescent blades and steel shafts. Many of the blades are fretted out in a design of arabesques incorporating the name of an Emir or with Koranic inscriptions. One type has a blade with a lower edge which extends downwards. The back of the axe is set with a quadrilateral projection for use as a hammer. Although many of these larger axes were carried as parade arms, some show the notched and damaged edges that indicate hard usage in war.

Another type of axe, often found in Persia, has a large crescent blade set at either side of the head, the surface of which is chiselled in the elaborate floral and figurative ornament of the Qajar period. Persian mounted warriors carried a distinctive type of small axe from the early Islamic period, according to literary sources[13]. A number of small axes with hatchet-shaped heads are preserved in collections. Most seem to date from the 17th or 18th century. The heads are small and the lower edge projects slightly down towards the handle which is usually of wood, sometimes with metal mounts. The surfaces are often finely chiselled and the back of the head terminates in a square platform. Some carry verses or the names of craftsmen. These are usually damascened in gold on the upper surface of the back. Unfortunately many of the saddle-axes are damaged or badly worn, and their inscriptions rarely survive.

Dr D. Nicolle has drawn attention to the illustration of a broad-bladed lance in the Automata Manuscript of 1206 by Al-Jazira, and broad-bladed lance heads of bronze are certainly known from the pre-Islamic period. The student and collector will generally encounter only detached lance heads usually of a period later than the 17th century. The blades are of several forms; either flat and narrow with a

13. Dr A.S. Melikian-Chirvani, 'The Tabarzins of Lotf 'Ali', p. 117, *Islamic Arms and Armour*, London 1979

43
Field Insignia
Engraved copper gilt
Turkish, last quarter of the
17th century
36 cm   933-1884

vestigial central rib, or a short type with a concave quadrilateral section. There are references to a two-pronged spear in some 12th-century epics from Persia. Some curious double-bladed lances with twin blades are preserved in Topkapi and other collections, all said to be of Persian origin. It is tempting to consider these as late survivors of this early form. They are either of very short, thick proportions with reinforced points, or long and flat with flamboyant blades. The latter are almost certainly parade arms. The blades extend into a substantial steel socket which fits onto the long wooden shaft. Many of the parade lances are of watered steel decorated with gold or silver damascening.

In the armouries of the Tower of London are some very short javelins of plain wood with triangular steel heads. Their provenance suggests that they came from the Arsenal at Rhodes and were captured from the Turks. The short javelin was usually employed for sport, especially in Persia and India. These generally come in sets of three in a wooden case, often mounted in silver. The more 'business-like' versions are of wood with long triangular-sectioned heads and flights. Some finely worked javelins made of tubular steel sections damascened in gold are known, probably of Persian origin. Their decoration is charactistic of 19th-century work.

Manuscripts sometimes illustrate warriors carrying long poles with a flat leaf-shaped blade at the top. These were military insignia and consisted of a flat sheet of metal, decorated with the insignia of a particular Emir, or bearing religious invocations. Egyptian forms from the 15th and 16th centuries have broad flat blades with pierced or engraved decoration; those from Persia were in the form of a circular disc extended into a leaf shape at the top. Some 16th-century Persian battle-standards are of pierced steel mounted in gilt brass. The entire surface is pierced with arabesques and inscriptions. A German woodcut of the late 17th century shows some captured Turkish metal standards which appear to be made in the form of flat boxes. Several of these are preserved among the collections of Turkish trophies in Eastern Europe. One example acquired in Egypt in the 19th century, constructed of copper, is decorated with inscriptions and flowers in a typical late Ottoman style. These standards served as a rallying-point for troops, and to identify forces.

It is gratifying to record that after many years of neglect scholars and collectors are showing an increasing interest in the arms and armour of Islam. The great variety of designs and types of weapon, superb workmanship and fine decoration are beginning to be appreciated, not only in Islamic lands but also in the West. Of great significance is the work of the scholars who are beginning to tackle the difficult problems of chronology and nationality posed by Islamic arms. This little book can only provide the briefest survey of an immense and complicated field. It is hoped that this general introduction, based upon the Victoria and Albert Museum's collection of Islamic arms, will stimulate readers not only to pursue this interesting field of study but also to look at the actual material.

Glossary

Arabesque — A type of design involving inter-laced foliate scrolls

Blunderbuss — A firearm with a distinctive flared muzzle

Capucines — Broad metal bands used to hold the barrel to the stock of a gun

Chape — The metal mount on a scabbard

Cock — A pivoting arm on a gun-lock in which the flint or pyrites are held

Damascening — A technique by which gold or silver are inlaid. Either gold or silver wire was hammered into an engraved design or, more commonly, the wire was fixed into a series of cross-hatched lines incised onto the surface

Eslabones — A combination tool used with Spanish firearms

Filigree — A decorative treatment involving the use of twisted silver wire

Flintlock — A type of gun-lock in which the sear operates vertically and the steel and pan-cover are made as one element

Full-cock — The position of the cock when ready to fire

Half-cock — The safety position of a cock, not fully pulled back against the mainspring

Janissaries — Specially trained troops of Muslim and Christian origin owing loyalty directly to the Turkish Sultan

Jezail — A type of long gun first used in Afghanistan

Kindjal — A broad straight double-edged knife used in the area of the Caucasus

Kaskara — A cross-hilted broadsword used in the Sudan

Lock plate — The flat plate to which the mecha-nism of a gun-lock is attached

Matchlock — A lock using burning match as a means of ignition

Mughal — A decorative style named after the ruling dynasty established in Northern India by Bābur (1526-30)

Niello — A black inlay formed of a mixture of lead, copper and silver sulphide

Pan-cover — The lid covering the pan on a gun-lock

Pommel — A large knob set at the end of a sword acting as a counter-balance to the weight of the blade

Powder tester — A device used to test the explosive power of gunpowder

Quillon — The cross-shaped guard of a sword

Rasak — A short gun used in the Balkans

Sear — A catch used in a gun-lock mecha-nism which engages with the cock and is released by the trigger

Sisana — A heavy gun based on Turkish prototypes popular in Bosnia and Serbia during the 18th century

Snaphance — A type of gun-lock in which the pan-cover and steel are made as separate elements

Spatulate — Flat and broad, shaped like a spatula

Steel — A pivoted steel plate which when struck by the flint causes sparks to fly into the pan

Tancica — A light gun used in the Balkan regions

Tang — The extension of the blade over which the handle fits

Toradar — A type of matchlock gun used in India

Tricker Matchlock — A matchlock firearm operated by a trigger

Tughra — An official Turkish stamp compris-ing the sultan's monogram and the formula 'ever Victorious'

Watered steel — A high-carbon steel used in the manufacture of sword-blades. When treated the surface exhibits a pattern resembling 'watered' silk

Wheel-lock — A type of gun-lock involving the use of a revolving grooved wheel

Wootz — A cake of high carbon content steel used in the manufacture of watered-steel sword blades

Yataghan — A type of short sword, with distinc-tive 'ears' on the grip, used in Turkey

Further Reading

The bibliography of Islamic arms is to date not extensive. Those readers new to the field will have to prepare themselves for some painstaking research in rather obscure journals. The following general works will provide useful information and are generally available at specialist bookshops or public libraries:

Lord Egerton of Tatton, *Indian and Oriental Armour*, Arms and Armour Press reprint, London 1968.

R. Elgood editor, *Islamic Arms and Armour*, London 1979. This has the advantage of containing an extensive modern bibliography.

Stone G.C., *A Glossary of the Construction, Decoration and Use of Arms and Armour in All Countries and All Times*, New York 1961. This is very useful but the reader needs to know the correct Eastern name for a particular weapon, to use the book quickly for reference purposes.

Vianello G., *Arma e Armature Orientale*, Milan 1966. This illustrates in colour a variety of Islamic arms, together with extensive captions.

For works on Islamic firearms, the following can be recommended. If not entirely devoted to Islamic gunsmiths's work, they nevertheless contain useful material:

Ayalon D., *Gunpowder and Firearms in the Mamluk Kingdom*, London 1956.

Blackmore H.L., *Guns and Rifles of the World*, London 1965.

Blair C., *Pistols of the World*, London 1968.

Blair C. editor, *Pollard's History of Firearms*, London 1983. This contains a comprehensive coverage of Islamic gunsmiths' work by Dr Zygulski.

Ivanov A., *Arts of Kubachi*, Leningrad 1976.

Information on the subject can also be found in catalogues. The following contain entries or are entirely devoted to Islamic arms.

Buttin C., *Collection d'Arms Anciennes*, Rumilly 1933.

Holstein P., *Armes Orientales*, Paris 1931.

Laking G.F., 'Oriental Arms and Armour', *Wallace Collection Catalogue*, London 1964.

Schöbel J., *Princely Arms and Armour*, London 1975.

Zeller R., and Rohrer E. F., *Orientalische Sammlung Henri Moser Charlottenfels* Berne 1955. This is a catalogue of a very large collection devoted to Islamic arms and armour.

The following exhibition catalogues contain relevant material.

Medeniveteri Anadolu, *Anatolian Civilisation*, Topkapi 1983.

Islamic Weapons in Danish Private Collections, Copenhagen 1982.

Atil E., *Art of the Mamluks*, Washington 1981.

Die Turken vor Vien, Vienna May 5th - Oct., 30th 1983. This describes Turkish and Persian arms used in the sieges of Vienna.

The following books deal with edged weapons only.

Rawson P.S., *The Indian Sword*, London 1968.

Seitz H., *Blankwaffen*, Brunswick 1968.

Wilkinson F., *Swords and Daggers*, London 1967.

Zaky A.R., *The Sword in Islam. Studies in Honour of Professor K.A.C. Creswell*, Cairo 1965.

Interesting Indian arms are illustrated in

Pant G.N. *Studies in Indian Weapons and Warfare* Delhi 1970.

For the more advanced student the following are detailed studies:

Nicolle D., *Early Medieval Islamic Arms and Armour*, Instituto de Estudios Sobre Armas Antiguas, Gladius, 1976.

Smith C.S., *A History of Metallography*, University of Chicago 1965. This has a very important chapter on watered steel as used in Islamic lands.

The only book on Islamic armourers' signatures and marks is:

Mayer L.A., *Islamic Armourers and Their Works*, Geneva 1962.

A general work on Islamic art which provides a background to the subject is:

Kuhnel E., *Islamic Arts*, Brunswick 1970.

For the arts of the Caucasus region, the following is a good introduction:

Chirkov D., *Daghestan Decorative Art*, Moscow 1971.

Interested parties should beg, borrow or steal a copy of the following bibliography which should give a very good grounding in the subject.

Creswell K.A.C., *Bibliography of Arms and Armour in Islam*, Royal Asiatic Society, London 1956.

Arms and armour journals occasionally publish

articles on Islamic material. Those listed below are the best known.

Arms Anciennes, Geneva
Armi Antiche, Turin
Arsenal, Cracow
Association Suisse Pour L'Étude des Armes, Geneva
Bulletin of the American Society of Arms Collectors, Dallas
Journal of the Arms and Armour Society, London
Livrustkammaren, Journal of the Royal Armoury, Stockholm
Svenska Vapenhistoriska Arsskrift, Copenhagen
Waffen- und Kostumkunde, Munich and Berlin